Discover India
State by State

OFF TO UTTAR PRADESH

SONIA MEHTA

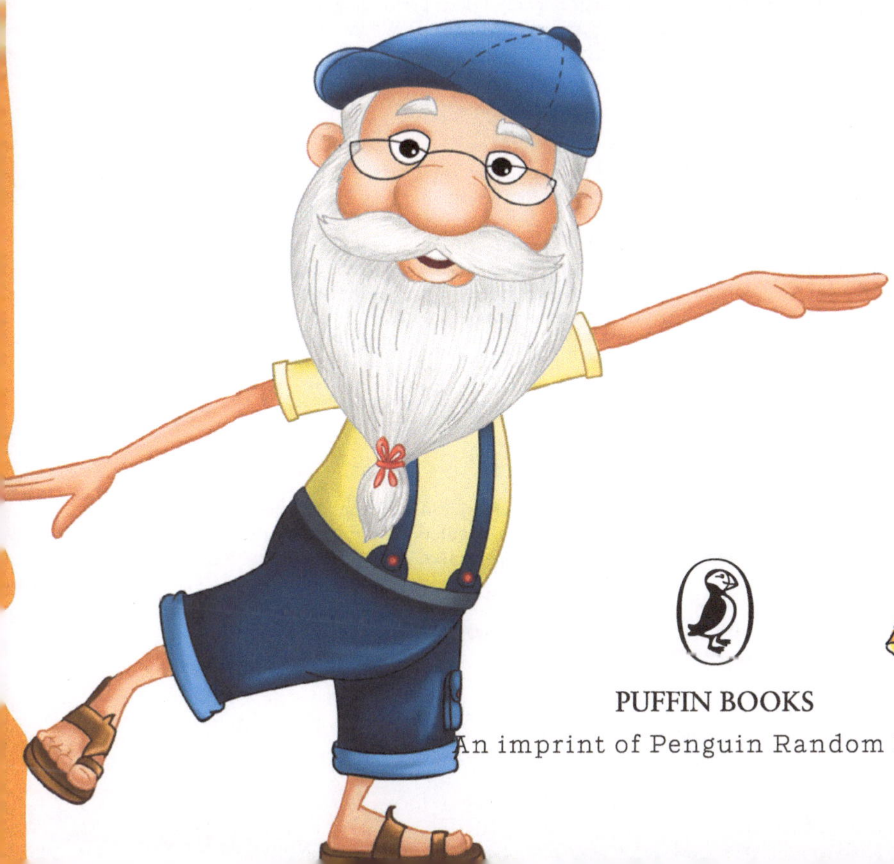

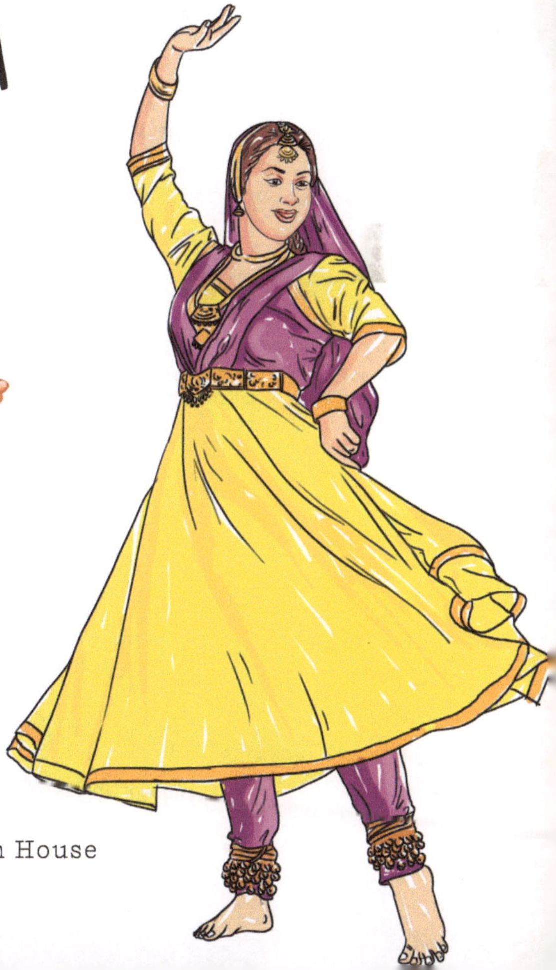

PUFFIN BOOKS
An imprint of Penguin Random House

PUFFIN BOOKS

USA | Canada | UK | Ireland | Australia | New Zealand | India | South Africa | China | Singapore

Puffin Books is part of the Penguin Random House group of companies whose addresses can be found at global.penguinrandomhouse.com

Published by Penguin Random House India Pvt. Ltd
4th Floor, Capital Tower 1, MG Road,
Gurugram 122 002, Haryana, India

First published in Puffin Books by Penguin Random House India 2017

Text, design and illustrations copyright © Quadrum Solutions Pvt. Ltd 2017
Series copyright © Penguin Random House India 2017

Picture Credits

P 7: Crowds in Kumbh Mela, Allahabad, Uttar Pradesh (Vladimir Melnik/Shutterstock.com); P 10: Ayodhya, Uttar Pradesh (Radiokafka/ Shutterstock.com); P 11: Allahabad, Uttar Pradesh (R.M. Nunes/Shutterstock.com); P 15: Wall art of Krishna and Arjun (reddees/Shutterstock. com); P 18: Bada Gaon Temple, Uttar Pradesh (© Capankajsmilyo (Own work) [CC BY-SA 4.0 (http://creativecommons.org/licenses/by-sa/4.0)], via Wikimedia Commons); P 25: Crowds at the Kumbh Mela (AJP/Shutterstock.com); P 26: Raaslila wall painting, Vrindavan, Uttar Pradesh (tantrik71/Shutterstock.com), Holi, Varanasi, Uttar Pradesh (Alexander Mazurkevich/Shutterstock.com); P 28: Ramlila performers (bodom/ Shutterstock.com); P 29: Nautanki performers (© Swagato Basumallick [CC BY-SA 3.0 (http://creativecommons.org/licenses/by-sa/3.0)], via Wikimedia Commons); P 30: Varanasi ghats (Sumit.Kumar.99/Shutterstock.com); P 34: Shahjahan and Mumtaz Mahal (Author Unknown [CC BY-SA 3.0 (http://creativecommons.org/licenses/by-sa/3.0)], via Wikimedia Commons); P 38: Royal Bath, Bara Imambara (saiko3p/Shutterstock. com), Staircase to the Royal bath, Bara Imambara (saiko3p/Shutterstock.com); P 40: Bullock cart (mundoview/Shutterstock.com); P 41: Chikan needlework (© Sonia Mehta); P 42: Taj Mahal complex (Dmitry Strizhakov/Shutterstock.com), Priests performing the Ganga arti (saiko3p/ Shutterstock.com); P 43: IT Park, Noida (© Sunil Kumar (Template: Skyscrapercity) [CC0], via Wikimedia Commons)

The views and opinions expressed in this book are the author's own and the facts are as reported by her, which have been verified to the extent possible, and the publishers are not in any way liable for the same.

The information in this book is based on research from bonafide sites and published books and is true to the best of the author's knowledge at the time of going to print. The author is not responsible for any further changes or developments occurring post the publication of this book. This series is not a comprehensive representation of the states of India but is intended to give children a flavour of the lifestyles and cultures of different states. All illustrations are artistic representations only.

ISBN 9780143440734

Design and layout by Quadrum Solutions Pvt. Ltd
Printed at Repro India Limited

www.penguin.co.in

This is a legitimate digitally printed version of the book and therefore might not
have certain extra finishing on the cover.

Hello Kids!

I'm so happy you are reading this book. India is an incredible country and there are lots of things about it that we never get to hear about.

I discovered India because my father was in the Indian army. He was posted to many places all over India—and we dutifully followed him. Can you imagine that by the time I was in the tenth standard, I had changed nine schools? Of course it was hard making new friends almost every year, but the good part was that I got to live in so many places. Right from Kerala, where I was born, to Kashmir, Jhansi, Shillong, Chandigarh, Goa . . . the list is long.

Every time I go to a new place, I feel amazed at how different each state is from the other—and yet, how similar. Did you know that we can see monuments from the Stone Age right here in India? Or that we have more than twenty official languages, and most Indians know three or four on an average? Or even that some of the world's most amazing scientific marvels were invented in India?

Oh, there are many, many, many fun and fantastic things about the states of India, which we simply must get to know.

So get your backpack ready, get set to meet some new friends and join me on a fun trip as we **DISCOVER INDIA, STATE BY STATE**.

I hope you enjoy reading this book as much as I have enjoyed writing it. I would love to hear from you. So do write to me at sonia.mehta@quadrumltd.com.

Lots of love,
Sonia Aunty

Mishki and Pushka have come to visit Earth from their home planet, Zoomba. They have never seen such an amazing place. Zoomba doesn't have trees and mountains and rivers like Earth does. But the people look exactly the same. When they come to Earth, they meet a sweet old man whom they call Daadu Dolma. Daadu Dolma shows them all the wonderful places in India and tells Mishki and Pushka all about them

Mishki and Pushka can't believe what they see. They have seen a lot of Earth, but they have never, ever seen a place like India.

They are off to explore India state by state :)

Mishki

Mishki is a curious little girl. She is always asking loads of questions. On her home planet, she is always getting into trouble for poking her nose into things that are not her business.

Pushka

Pushka is Mishki's brother. He **loves adventure**. He is always ready to try a new challenge. Whether it's climbing a mountain, or diving into a cold, cold sea, he is up for it.

Daadu Dolma

Daadu Dolma is a wise old man who has lived on Earth longer than the mountains and seas. No one knows quite how old he is, but he certainly has been around. He knows everything about everything.

Mishki and Pushka can't believe what a big country India is.

'Where are we going next, Daadu Dolma?' asks Pushka.

'We are going to a very, very interesting state,' replies Daadu Dolma. 'It's a state whose history is literally the history of India.'

'Wow,' says Mishki. 'It must be a very old state then.'

'Yes, it is. It is very old. And full of amazing things,' says Daadu Dolma. 'So get set to discover the amazing state of Uttar Pradesh.'

Mishki and Pushka clap their hands in delight.

OFF TO UTTAR PRADESH!!!

A SNEAK PEEK

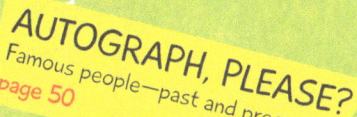

Land ahoy!

Look, Daadu Dolma, Uttar Pradesh has no sea around it.

That's right, Pushka. Uttar Pradesh is surrounded by land.

Knock Knock Knock

SO MANY NEXT-DOOR NEIGHBOURS

Uttar Pradesh has many Indian states as next-door neighbours. There's Bihar to the east; Chhattisgarh and Jharkhand to the south-east; Madhya Pradesh to the south; Rajasthan, Delhi, Himachal Pradesh and Haryana to the west; and Uttarakhand, as well as the country of Nepal, to the north. Wow! No one in Uttar Pradesh can ever be lonely!

ON THE MAP

To see exactly where Uttar Pradesh is on the map of India, go to http://www.mapsofindia.com/maps/india/india-political-map.htm

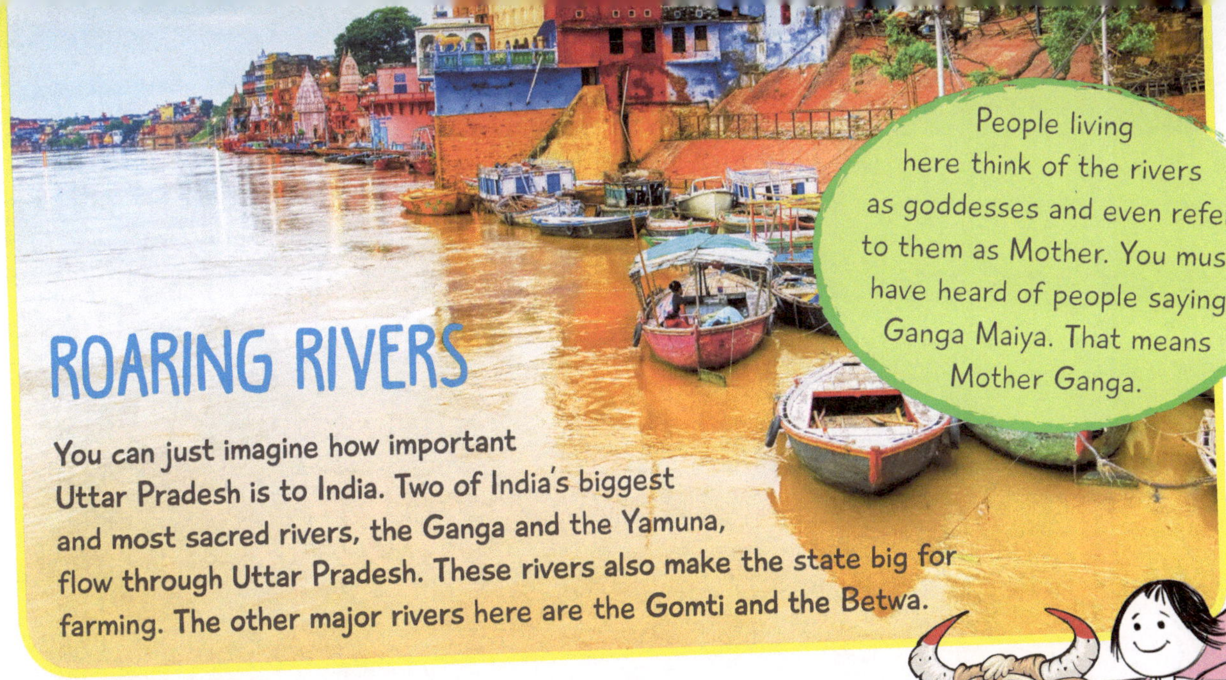

ROARING RIVERS

You can just imagine how important Uttar Pradesh is to India. Two of India's biggest and most sacred rivers, the Ganga and the Yamuna, flow through Uttar Pradesh. These rivers also make the state big for farming. The other major rivers here are the Gomti and the Betwa.

People living here think of the rivers as goddesses and even refer to them as Mother. You must have heard of people saying Ganga Maiya. That means Mother Ganga.

Did you know?
Uttar Pradesh is a part of India's Cow Belt.

It is called so because it is rich in agriculture and livestock.

OH, SO CROWDED!

Uttar Pradesh is India's fifth largest state but is the most populated. The population of Uttar Pradesh is more than the whole of Brazil. Whoa!

TOUCHING THE FOOT OF THE HIMALAYAS

Though there are lots of agricultural plains, the northern part of Uttar Pradesh touches the foothills of the magnificent Himalayan mountain range. The Sivalik Hills run through here. It's a wonderful, cool, beautiful place.

The Indo-Gangetic Plain is rich in fertile soil.

PLAINS, PLATEAUS AND MOUNTAINS

Uttar Pradesh has all three. But most of the state is covered by a flat land called the Indo-Gangetic Plain. It's called this because the river Ganga has made the entire area rich, fertile and perfect for farming.

HOT AND COLD AND WET

Like a lot of India, Uttar Pradesh has three main seasons. Cold, cold winters; hot, hot summers; and wet, wet monsoons. But different parts of the state have different temperatures at the same time. When it snows in the Himalayas, it can get freezing cold. But summers can be hot and dry, leaving you feeling like a baked potato.

Farmers wait for the rains, which arrive between June and September.

HOT OR COLD

Mishki wants to know what the weather will be. Can you fill in the blank space with sun or clouds by following the patterns?

A

B

C

D

9

CITYSCAPES

Uttar Pradesh has some of India's most historically important cities. Do you know why? Because so much of India's history and mythology originated here. Let's go and visit some cities of Uttar Pradesh.

Ayodhya is the city where Lord Rama was born and lived as a king.

AYODHYA

AGRA

LUCKNOW

VARANASI

Lucknow is the capital city of Uttar Pradesh. It used to be the seat of power for the nawabs more than 200 years ago.

Varanasi is a famous holy city on the bank of the Ganga. People from all over the world come here to take a dip.

Agra sits on the banks of the Yamuna River. See the Taj Mahal?

VRINDAVAN

ALLAHABAD

Vrindavan is where the much-loved Lord Krishna is supposed to have lived.

Allahabad is famous for the Kumbh Mela. It's also where the famous actor Amitabh Bachchan was born.

CITYSEARCH

Help Pushka find the cities and rivers from Uttar Pradesh. He wants to visit them all.

```
A L A G O M T I A W
V R I N D A V A N F
A G E R M Y W E E V
R A X Y N O X C V N
A N V G W D Z C C V
N G Z N J H A N S I
A A E B A Y F H G M
S T Q R Y A G R A N
I L U C K N O W K U
C Y A M U N A R R W
```

WILD AND WONDERFUL

Time for adventure! Let's see the amazing wildlife in Uttar Pradesh. Would you believe that there are over fifty types of mammals in Uttar Pradesh? Sadly, almost half of these are endangered. There are tigers, antelope, deer, wild boar, elephants and rhinoceroses roaming the forests.

They are in danger!

Some of the creatures that are endangered are wild dogs, tigers, leopards, Gangetic dolphins and Asian elephants. The government is trying its best to save these animals by protecting them in wildlife sanctuaries.

ANIMAL PROTECTION

KEEPING THEM SAFE

There are many, many wildlife sanctuaries in Uttar Pradesh. The Dudhwa National Park is one of the most famous. It has three large forests and several small lakes and swamps. Many animals roam safely here, including majestic Bengal tigers, one-horned rhinoceroses and cheetahs. Various rare species of birds live here too.

Sorry, Mishki, but according to my GPS-receiver, I am still in my own territory . . .

FUN FACT

State bird
Sarus crane

State animal
Barasingha

State flower
Palash

State tree
Ashoka

Long, long ago

That's because the history of Uttar Pradesh is literally the history of India.

Wow, Daadu Dolma, there are so many old buildings here. Why is that?

THE CRADLE OF INDIAN CIVILIZATION

Thousands and thousands of years ago, the area that we now call Uttar Pradesh was the home of the Aryans. It is believed that they came to India from Greece and other parts of Europe through the Himalayas. They were looking to conquer new lands and build new kingdoms. India was perfect for what they were seeking.

Did you know?
It was in this region that the ancient epics the Mahabharata and the Ramayana were written.

Arjun

Lord Krishna

KINGS AND KINGDOMS

The kingdom of Hastinapur is where all the action began. According to legend, King Pandu had five sons—the Pandavas. His brother, Dhritarashtra, who was blind, had 100 sons. The cousins fought for the throne in a great battle that has gone down in history as the Battle of Kurukshetra. (Kurukshetra is now in the state of Haryana.) The Pandavas won and ruled the land for many years.

Do It Yourself
Word Ladder

Help Pushka climb the word ladder by changing one letter in each word as he climbs it.

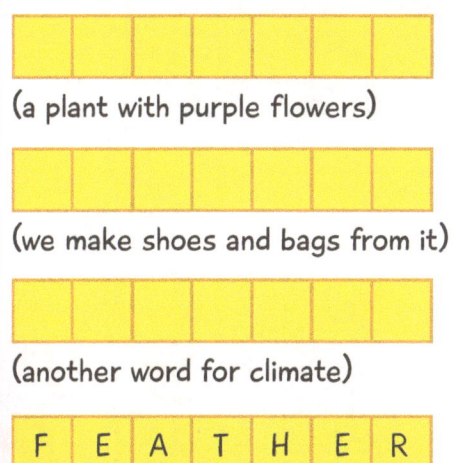

(a plant with purple flowers)

(we make shoes and bags from it)

(another word for climate)

| F | E | A | T | H | E | R |

THE GOD WITH A PEACOCK FEATHER

Millions of people across the world worship Lord Krishna. He was known to be a god who had the answers to everything. He was born in Mathura in Uttar Pradesh. There are lots of stories about his mischief, his bravery and his wisdom. He was born to the Yadav clan, who were one of the ruling families during that time. It is said that he always wore a peacock feather in his hair.

How cool!

SO MANY RULERS

Anyone who wanted to invade India had to come through the mountains and pass through the Indo-Gangetic Plain, as the rest of India was surrounded by sea. Because of this, Uttar Pradesh saw many rulers that came, conquered and ruled, until they were defeated by the next invaders.

The different dynasties that ruled over this region were the Vatsas, Kosis, Hosalas, Videhs and, finally, the Nandas.

POWER TO THE MAURYAS

The Mauryas were a powerful dynasty. They defeated the Nandas, who were ruling at that time, but they did not stop at that. Under their powerful and clever king, Chandragupta Maurya, they spread their kingdom into many other parts of India.

Great rulers entering and conquering different parts of India.

THE LEGACY OF CHANDRAGUPTA MAURYA

Chandragupta Maurya was as wise as he was powerful. His kingdom spread across India, except the part that is now Tamil Nadu. He even defeated Alexander's armies, who tried their best to enter India. Then, he set about organizing things. He made rules that were fair to people. He helped farmers and traders. He built ties with the Western world. Life was good under Chandragupta Maurya's rule.

Did you know?
In Greek history, Chandragupta is referred to as Sandrokottos.

Hidden Words

There are many smaller words hidden inside the name

CHANDRAGUPTA MAURYA.

How many can you make?

_____
_____
_____
_____
_____
_____

JAINISM SPREADS

At this time, a spiritual movement was beginning. A great saint called Bhagvan Mahavir was born. He started the religion called Jainism. Some of the greatest saints of Jainism (also called tirthankaras) were from Uttar Pradesh. Bada Gaon Temple is a famous Jain temple in Uttar Pradesh.

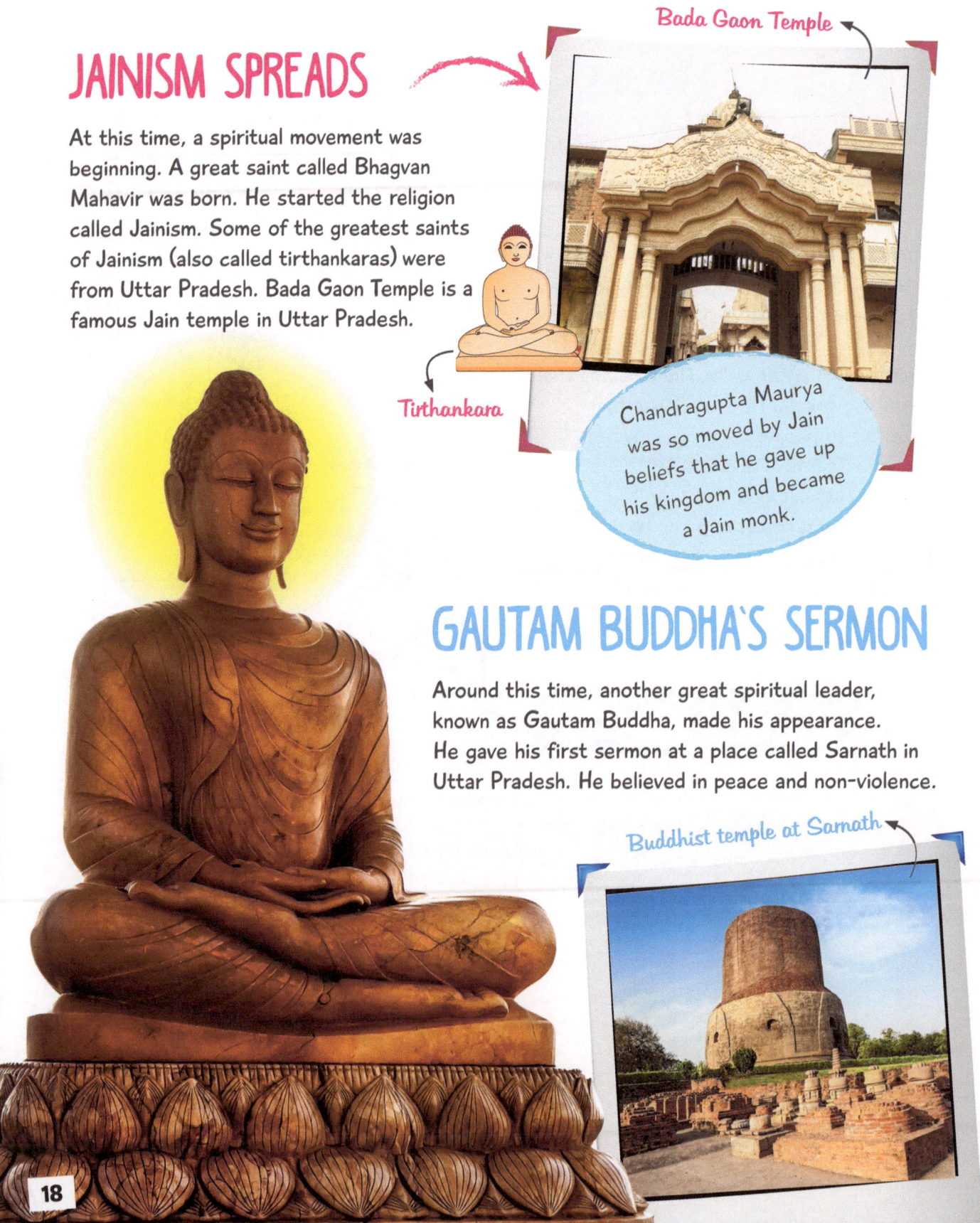

Bada Gaon Temple

Tirthankara

Chandragupta Maurya was so moved by Jain beliefs that he gave up his kingdom and became a Jain monk.

GAUTAM BUDDHA'S SERMON

Around this time, another great spiritual leader, known as Gautam Buddha, made his appearance. He gave his first sermon at a place called Sarnath in Uttar Pradesh. He believed in peace and non-violence.

Buddhist temple at Sarnath

THE LIFE OF KING ASHOKA

Ashoka was the son of King Bindusara and grandson of Chandragupta Maurya. He was known for his bravery and ruthlessness. Once, during a battle, he saw thousands of young soldiers die painful deaths. He saw the grief of their families. He was horrified. From that day on, he began to follow Buddha's teachings. He gave up war and began to spread the message of peace. He ordered his people to inscribe Buddha's teachings on rocks, pillars and temples. These are visible even today.

King Ashoka preaching Buddha's teachings

Did you know?

The Ashoka Stambh (which means pillar) is India's national emblem. King Ashoka built nineteen such pillars. The main one is at Sarnath in Uttar Pradesh. It has four lions with their backs to each other. The lions are symbols of power, courage, confidence and pride.

BUDDHA'S FOOTPRINTS

These footprints are found in many parts of Uttar Pradesh. Can you draw them on a piece of paper? All the symbols have different meanings. Find out what they all mean.

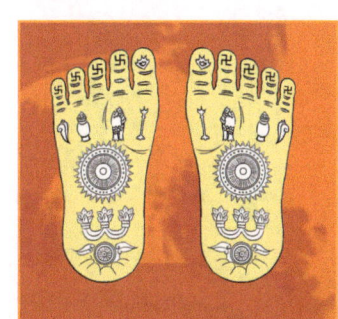

RUN, RUN! THE HUNS ARE COMING!

The Huns were a bloodthirsty warrior clan who invaded India from the north. They marched into the peaceful Gupta territory many times. At first, the Guptas were able to defeat them. But finally, the Huns were the reason why the Gupta Empire ended.

The Huns were unruly and did not do much for either Uttar Pradesh or the other areas that they conquered.

THE MUGHALS ARRIVE

Many years later, after several skirmishes and attempts by other kings, the Mughals arrived from Central Asia, where they had been busy conquering lands. A powerful king called Babur defeated all that came in his way, and soon the Mughal Empire was established in India. After Babur, his son Humayun and grandson Akbar became the Mughal emperors. Akbar made Agra his capital city.

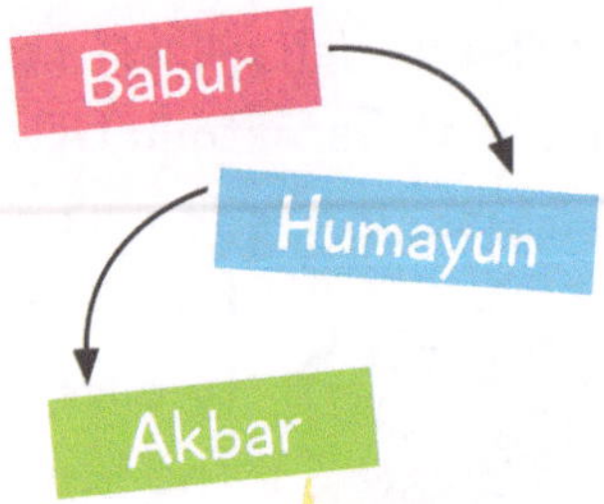

Babur

Humayun

Akbar

A GOLDEN AGE

Akbar was a great king. He conquered almost all of India. He built magnificent forts and palaces in Agra and Allahabad. After him, his son Jehangir and grandson Shahjahan continued his good work. There was wonderful art, beautiful architecture and refined culture that developed during their reign. It was Shahjahan who built the magnificent Taj Mahal in Agra, in memory of his wife Mumtaz Mahal. Shahjahan built many monuments all over northern India, including the Red Fort in Delhi.

THE END OF THE MUGHALS

The Mughal rule began to decline. Aurangzeb took over from Shahjahan, but his son Bahadur was weak. Other smaller kings began to set up their own kingdoms. Soon, India was scattered. It was perfect for the British, who took charge after defeating various smaller kings and capturing kingdoms.

The Red Fort at Agra

Details inside the Taj Mahal

WE WANT TO BE FREE

A lot of people from Uttar Pradesh fought the British for freedom. In fact, many of India's greatest freedom fighters were from this region (it was not yet a state, you see). The Sepoy Mutiny took place in Meerut. The Chauri Chaura incident, in which angry crowds burnt a police station, also occurred in Uttar Pradesh. It was after India became independent in 1947 that Uttar Pradesh finally became the state we know.

Talk time

Adaab, Daadu Dolma.

What does that mean?

Where did you learn that? That is a lovely way of saying hello in Urdu.

PURE FOR SURE

The official language of Uttar Pradesh is Hindi. In fact, Uttar Pradesh is part of India's Hindi Belt. But there are many types of Hindi that the people speak here. Khari Boli is the most used and what people use in their everyday conversations.

A lovely mix of Hindi and Urdu is the Hindustani language. It sounds very pure and elegant.

Hello

Urdu.......... Salaam alaikum
Hindi.......... Namaste
Bhojpuri.... Pranaam

Goodbye

Urdu.......... Khuda hafiz
Hindi.......... Alvida
Bhojpuri.... Ram ram

Welcome

Urdu.......... Khushamdeed
Hindi.......... Swagat hai
Bhojpuri.... Aain na

Happy Birthday

Urdu.......... Saalgirah mubarak
Hindi.......... Janam din ki shubh kaamna
Bhojpuri.... Janamdin mubarak

SAME BUT DIFFERENT

There are other languages too that are a mix of Hindi and other dialects, like Bhojpuri. It sounds a lot like Hindi but is different. Then there's Awadhi. This is from the Awadh region of Uttar Pradesh. And finally, there's Braj Bhasha, the language Lord Krishna is supposed to have spoken.

MATCH THE WORDS

Match the words with the same meaning. Oh wow! You are learning new languages.

Salaam alaikum	Khushamdeed
Janamdin mubarak	Alvida
Aain na	Khuda hafiz
Khuda hafiz	Pranaam
Ram ram	Saalgirah mubarak

The second language spoken here is Urdu. Urdu is a result of mixing Hindi and Persian, the language that the Mughals spoke. It is the favourite language of writers and poets because of its delicacy and expressiveness.

A peep into their life

Daadu, I want to know how people live in Uttar Pradesh. Are they different in any way?

No Mishki. They are not different. But they are not exactly the same either.

THE CRADLE OF HINDUISM

Lord Rama and Lord Krishna, among India's most loved and famous gods, are from Uttar Pradesh. No wonder millions come here every year. Varanasi, which is one of India's oldest cities, has millions of visitors and tourists. Hindus comprise the largest number of people in Uttar Pradesh. Quite a few people here are religious, and you will see lots of priests and sadhus on the streets of Uttar Pradesh's towns.

In the style of the nawabs

The nawabs were Muslim royalty. They left behind a unique way of life and culture. Even today, you will see many people living this lifestyle. Muslims are the second largest group of people in Uttar Pradesh.

THE LARGEST GATHERING IN THE WORLD

Once every twelve years, millions and millions of people gather together in Allahabad for the Kumbh Mela. This is where the three holy rivers, Ganga, Yamuna and Saraswati, meet. It is called the Triveni Sangam. It is such a large gathering that it is said that it can be seen from outer space. **Imagine that!**

Daadu, you are talking in riddles.

TWIN SADHUS

There are so many sadhus here. Mishki is confused. Can you help her find two sadhus who are exactly the same?

A   B   C   D   E   F

MUSIC

FOLKSY TUNES

You could call Uttar Pradesh the land of hermits, sages, kings, emperors and nawabs. It is also the land of ancient hymns, mantras, poetry and culture. Because of this, it has an amazing and rich tradition of music and dance. There are many styles of folk music. Here are just two popular styles out of a long list.

Rasiya
This is sung in Braj Bhasha. The songs are about Lord Krishna being playful with the village maidens.

Chaiti
This is a seasonal style, sung mainly during spring and the festivals of Holi and Ramnavami.

GOING CLASSICAL

Oh gosh! There's so much music in this area. Some of India's greatest classical music forms were born here, thanks to the kings and emperors who supported musicians in their courts.

Thumri
This style of singing is a mix of folk and classical music. It is very refined, and the words are often to do with Lord Krishna's love for Radha.

Gazals
The gazal is actually a short poem that is set to music. Originally, it came through the Mughals, who brought it with them from Persia.

Hindustani classical music
This style, which flourished in Uttar Pradesh, is called the Banarasi Gharana. Men who are masters in this are called Pandit (if Hindu) or Ustad (if Muslim). Women get the status of Bai or Begum.

GREAT MUSICIANS

Uttar Pradesh has given India some of its greatest musicians. Let's meet some of them.

Tansen
Although he was born in Gwalior, Madhya Pradesh, the great musician served in Emperor Akbar's court.

Begum Akhtar
She is known to have a magical voice.

Pandit Hariprasad Chaurasia
He is one of the most famous flautists in India.

Shubha Mudgal
She is considered to be a thumri expert.

DANCE AND DRAMA

Just like music, Uttar Pradesh has given birth to some famous folk and classical dance forms that are now performed all over India.

RAMLILA

Ramlila is a fun folk play in which people enact the story of Lord Rama. The actors dress up in colourful costumes. The entire village comes to see the play. It is usually performed during the Dussehra festival, to celebrate Ram's victory over Raavan, an evil king. It's great fun to see the actors dressed to the hilt with loud make-up to look their part.

KATHAK

This is a lovely dance form that used to be performed in the courts of the Mughal kings. Kathak dancers are nimble on their feet and are very expressive too.

NAUTANKI

This is an engrossing folk theatre style of art. There are actors and singers who take part. The story is often based on mythological stories. In Uttar Pradesh's villages, nautanki performances sometimes go on through the night. That's how much people enjoy it.

ARTISTES AND THEIR ART

The people of Uttar Pradesh have always been very artistic. The art from this state is famous all over the world, right from the beautiful rock paintings of pre-historic times to today's miniatures, pottery, jewellery and metal work.

ODD ONE OUT

As usual, Mishki wants to solve the riddle. In each of the rows below, one word is out of place. Circle it and help Mishki.

Jewellery	Pottery	Miniature painting	Sports
Nautanki	Ramlila	Gazal	Kathak
Gazal	Thumri	Nautanki	Bhajan
Rama	Krishna	Buddha	Ashoka

Bricks and stones

Today, Uttar Pradesh is a mix of simple villages and big, modern cities. So there's a lot of simple living alongside modern life.

Where do people live in Uttar Pradesh? I want to see.

VILLAGE CHARM

Most of the people of Uttar Pradesh live in villages. A typical village is made of groups of mud huts with mud roads between the houses. The roofs are often made of straw or thatch. As you go closer to the cities, the villages become slightly more modern, with tiles, paved streets and more modern gadgets in their simple homes—like TVs and refrigerators.

A WONDERFUL POTPOURRI

Most cities in Uttar Pradesh are an interesting hotchpotch. In the middle of busy streets, with shops, food stalls and traffic honking and screeching around, you will suddenly see a magnificent gate or pillar that is thousands of years old. There are mosques, shrines and temples that dot the cities. Some cities have palaces that are in semi-ruin.

THE GHATS OF THE GANGA

Varanasi—which used to be called Banaras—has a completely different style of architecture. The star attraction is, of course, the Ganga. Millions visit it every year. They believe a dip in the cold river water helps to purify them.

There are wide stone steps leading to the river. These are called the **ghats**. There are also lots of small and large temples devoted to different gods dotting this area.

SONG BY THE RIVER

A woman is sitting by the ghats of the Ganga. Can you spot seven differences in the two images?

Standing strong

Daadu, I have never seen such beautiful buildings. What are they?

The kings of Uttar Pradesh built some amazing monuments. Come, let's visit some.

The Rumi Darwaza used to be the gateway to Lucknow city hundreds of years ago. It is supposed to be exactly like the gateway to Constantinople, which is why it is also called Turkish Gateway.

It is a massive structure through which vehicles pass today.

THE OLD AND THE NEW

Lucknow's main market, called Hazratganj, is a wonderful mix of ancient and modern architecture. There are lovely pebbled pathways, wrought iron lampposts and lots of greenery. You can tell that the British were here.

THE BUDDHIST TEMPLES IN SARNATH

Sarnath, the place where Gautam Buddha gave his first sermon, has many beautiful Buddhist temples. The main temple is the Sarnath Temple. All the temples have lots of inscriptions, many of which were ordered by Emperor Ashoka.

Ruins of early temples and Buddhist stupas of the ancient city of Sarnath

That's a lot of windows! Let me count by rows.

WINDOW DRESSING

Can you count the number of window arches in this monument? Pushka wants to get inside each of them.

THE FAMOUS TAJ MAHAL

Emperor Shahjahan, of the Mughal Empire, was deeply in love with his wife Mumtaz Mahal. When she died, he decided to build a tomb so that the world would forever know how much he loved her. And so, he built the beautiful Taj Mahal.

It took close to twenty-two years to build, and nearly 20,000 workers worked day and night to build it. More than 1000 elephants carried the marble and stones that were used to build it.

There are ninety-nine names of Allah that have been inscribed on the sides of Mumtaz Mahal's tomb.

Wow! The Taj Mahal is the most wonderful monument we have ever seen!

AGRA FORT

Close to the Taj Mahal is Agra Fort. It's made of red sandstone, so people also call it Red Fort or Lal Quila. People are so impressed with the Taj Mahal that they forget how amazing Agra Fort is. There's a Hall of Mirrors—a room made of millions of tiny pieces of mirror. There's a huge courtyard, where the ladies used to hold their bazaars. There's even a tower, where Emperor Shahjahan was made prisoner for eight long years. From one small window, he could see the Taj Mahal far away.

The Peacock Throne in Agra Fort was made of millions of precious stones, including the magnificent Kohinoor diamond, which now sits on the British Crown.

COUNT THE DIAMONDS

Mishki has never seen so many diamonds. Can you help her count how many diamonds there are in this figure? One has been marked for you.

FABULOUS FORT

A furious battle was fought between Rani Laxmibai of Jhansi and the British at Jhansi Fort. It is said that she strapped her baby son to her back and leapt from the high turrets of the fort to escape from the British, rather than be imprisoned by them.

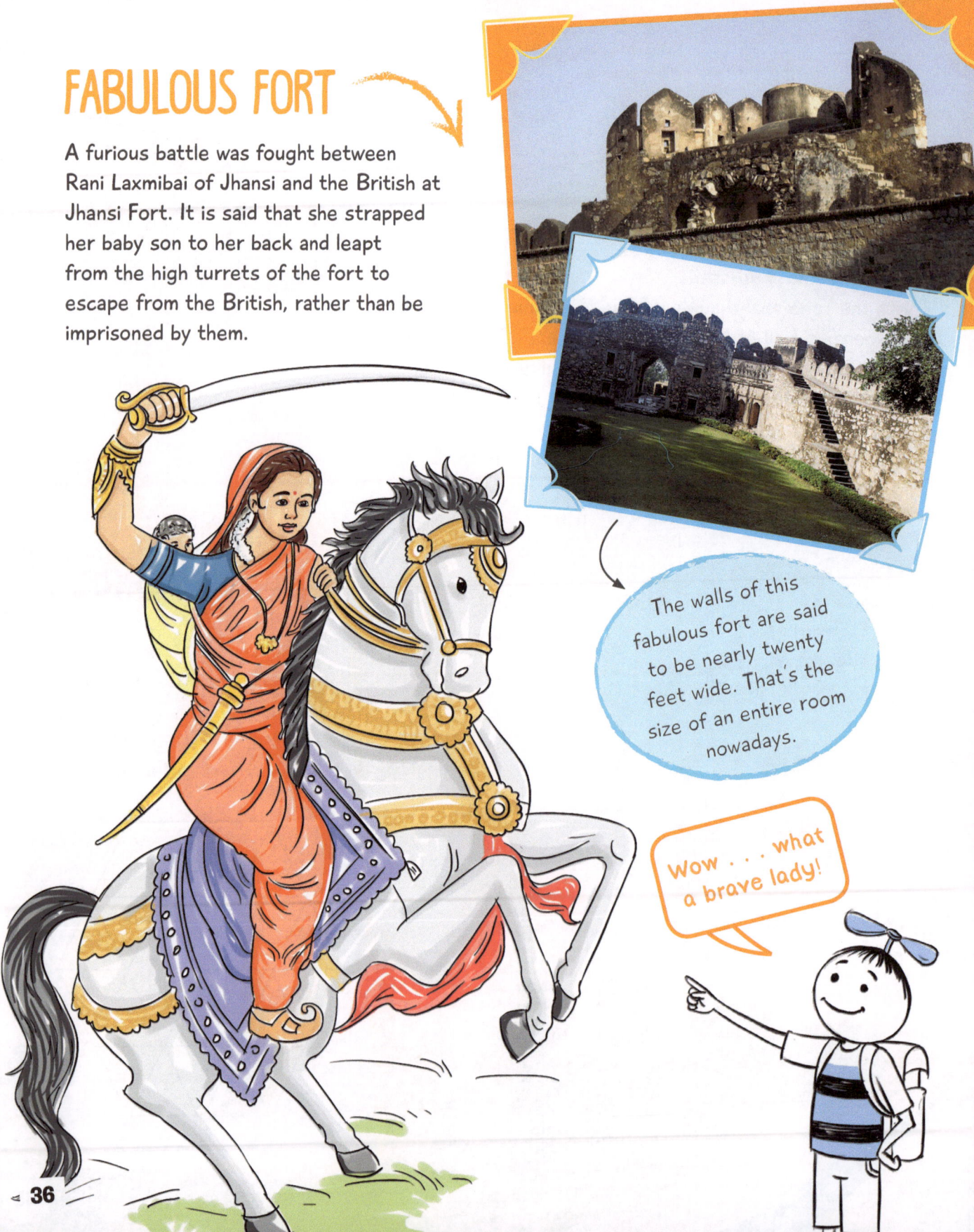

The walls of this fabulous fort are said to be nearly twenty feet wide. That's the size of an entire room nowadays.

Wow . . . what a brave lady!

Intricate carvings on the stupa

DHAMEK STUPA

This stupa was built on another structure that had been built by King Ashoka after he became a devout Buddhist. It is in Sarnath, where Buddha gave his first sermon. Over the years, it has been made bigger and taller. There are intricate floral, human and bird carvings on the stupa. There are also writings carved on it in the Brahmi script, the script used by the Mauryas.

Khusro Bagh

A MAGNIFICENT TOMB

Khusro Bagh is where Prince Khusro, Emperor Jehangir's son, was buried. Today, it is a beautiful walled garden with arches. His mother and sister's tombs are also here. Can you imagine that poor Prince Khusro was imprisoned by his own brother, who wanted to make sure that he became king? What cruel times those must have been.

FATEHPUR SIKRI

This is actually a small city built by Emperor Akbar. Its name means the City of Victory. It is a complex made of temples, mosques and monuments. The famous Jama Masjid, one of India's largest mosques, is here. The entire city was made of red sandstone. It has a complicated drainage system too.

One of the most amazing structures is the Panch Mahal—a five-storied structure built to catch the wind.

Guess who lived here? Birbal, Akbar's witty minister.

BARA IMAMBARA

The Bara Imambara was built by a nawab called Asaf-ud-Daula. It is famous for its labyrinth (called Bhool Bhulaiya) and its hall, which is one of the largest of its kind in the world. Now, it is used by Shia Muslims for their mourning ceremonies.

Royal bath at Bara Imambara

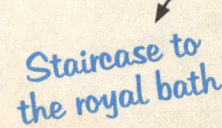
Staircase to the royal bath

THE CHOTA IMAMBARA

The Chota Imambara isn't small like its name suggests. It was built by another nawab called Muhammad Ali Shah. It has lots of beautiful chandeliers, domes and intricate carvings. It also has the tombs of Muhammad Ali Shah and his mother.

The chandeliers in the Chota Imambara are super cool!

ROYAL MAZE

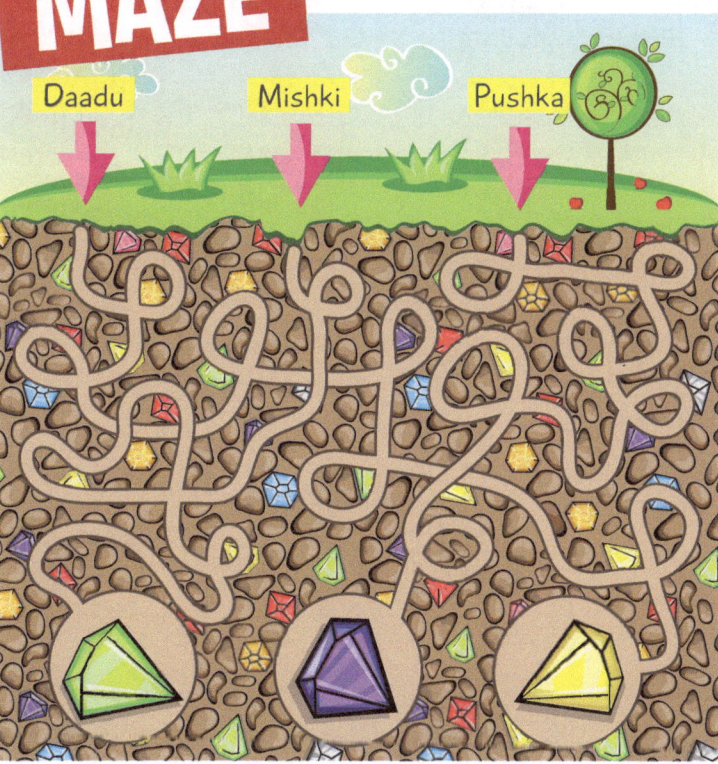

Daadu   Mishki   Pushka

Mishki, Pushka and Daadu Dolma have gone on a diamond hunt. See who finds which diamond!

Working hard

How do people earn money in Uttar Pradesh, Daadu?

People have to work hard for a living, Mishki. Come, let's find out what they do!

Did you know? Most of India's livestock (that means cows, buffaloes and other animals used in farming) comes from Uttar Pradesh.

SUGAR AND SPICE AND EVERYTHING NICE

Because of the Indo-Gangetic Plain, lots of crops grow in Uttar Pradesh. Guess what farmers here grow the most? Sugar cane! Of course, there are lots of other crops that grow here too. Like pulses, wheat, rice, potatoes and oil seeds.

SMALL BUT BEAUTIFUL

It feels like everyone here is talented. Uttar Pradesh's cottage industries are so, so famous. There are lots and lots of skilled craftsmen. Just see all that they make.

The weavers of Banaras create magic with the Banarasi sari, which has pure gold thread woven in.

Lucknow is famous for its Chikan embroidery—a detailed style of needlework that is beautiful and much loved.

The skilled potters of Khurja make incredible ceramics with their nimble fingers.

The brass work of Moradabad is known all over the world.

WELCOMING ALL TOURISTS

Think about how many world famous monuments are in Uttar Pradesh. No wonder that tourism is a big, big industry here. Thanks to the millions of tourists that visit this state, thousands of people work in hotels, airlines and other jobs that have to do with showing visitors the beauty and history of this state.

The Taj Mahal is one of the most photographed monuments in the world.

Priests performing the Ganga Puja, which is an important tourist attraction in Varanasi.

Tourism is one of the biggest industries in Uttar Pradesh.

TECHIE LAND

Although Uttar Pradesh is so historic, it isn't being left behind in modern times. Noida is an ultra-modern city that has been specially built with super cool technology and infrastructure. It is so close to Delhi that lots of people who work in Delhi live here. Many big technology companies, banks and medicine companies have their offices here.

IT park in Noida, Uttar Pradesh

Thousands of people live and work here. It has amazing technology and infrastructure too.

TOURIST TRICK

This tourist guide has decided to show Mishki and Pushka the Taj Mahal. But it's too dark. Can you help them match the correct shadow of the Taj Mahal?

1 2 3

4 5 6

Yum yum yum

Now my favourite part! My tummy's rumbling already.

In that case, you had better get ready to eat some of India's most amazing food.

Jalebi

SO RICH, SO DIFFERENT

The kings and emperors loved to hunt and eat meat. The royal kitchens made some amazing food that is now known around the world as Mughlai food. On the other hand, the pure vegetarian food of Mathura and Vrindavan is just as popular and famous.

COOLEST KEBABS

You'll get to taste all kinds of kebabs here. These are pieces of meat grilled on skewers. Today, these kebabs are famous all over the world.

OFF THE STREETS

Everyone loves Banarasi food. You find this on the streets of Uttar Pradesh, as well as in traditional homes. Jalebis, kachauris and samosas have made their way across India.

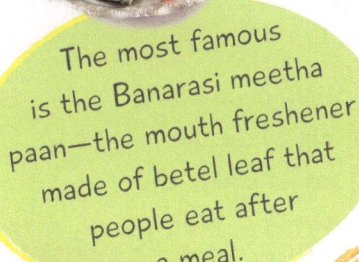
Mutton kebabs

Meetha paan

The most famous is the Banarasi meetha paan—the mouth freshener made of betel leaf that people eat after a meal.

Kachauris

Samosa

Mmm . . . yummm!

OOH! BIRYANI

In the Awadh part of Uttar Pradesh, people had a special way of cooking rice mixed with meat. It was called dum pukht. The rice and meat are packed tightly in vessels that are sealed with flour. Then the vessel is placed on a low flame and cooked for hours and hours. This kind of biryani is a speciality of Lucknow.

THE HANDKERCHIEF BREAD

No, no! This isn't really anyone's hanky. It's just a roti (or bread) that is so thin that it folds like a handkerchief. It was invented during Mughal times. Watching someone make it is as much fun as eating it is. The cook twirls the flour up in the air and it comes flying down to rest on a griddle, on which it is cooked. This is the famous roomali roti.

YELLOW RIVER

A nawab called Wajid Ali Shah loved pomp and ceremony. During spring, when the flowers turned yellow, he would order the river Gomti to be coloured yellow. Women would dance and everyone would celebrate. During this time, the royal cooks would make a yummy dish called zarda. This is a delicious mix of rice, milk, raisins and saffron that makes the dish as yellow as the river.

A swirl, a twirl and the roomali roti is ready!

Yummy zarda with raisins and saffron

What a feast!!!

BREAD WITH A DIFFERENCE

There's a yummy bread called sheermal that is a speciality in parts of Uttar Pradesh. It is cooked like bread in an oven, and people love to eat it with meats and curries. Did you know that sheermal is also eaten in other countries, like Iran, which have the Persian influence?

Delicious sheermal eaten with curries

CRACK THE FOOD CODE

Pushka is so hungry. There's something written on the menu that he can't understand. Help him crack the code and find the name of the yummy dish.

1 = Y	3 = H	7 = B	10 = A
2 = U	6 = O	9 = I	12 = N
4 = M	5 = T	8 = R	

1 2 4 4 1   3 6 5   7 9 8 1 10 12 9

What to wear?

Why are you looking so different, Pushka? What is it that you are wearing?

I have decided that I am a king in Uttar Pradesh. This is how I am going to dress.

DRESSED FOR A WEDDING

The traditional clothing for men during the Mughal era was a long, elaborate coat that they wore over tights (or churidar). Now, men wear it only to weddings or festivals. Women, on the other hand, wore pyjamas and long flowing tops that almost reached their ankles. These too are worn by women to weddings today.

A SIMPLE DHOTI AND KURTA

Today, especially in villages, men wear short, loose kurtas over dhotis or lungis. So much easier. The dhoti is also worn in other parts of India. It has many different names too, like veshti, mardani, chaadra and pancha.

SARI OR SKIRT?

The women in villages wear either a sari or a long skirt with a top. They cover their head with a loose cloth called a ghungat.

GOING MODERN

Of course, in most Indian cities and small towns, everyone dresses alike. Men in jeans and shirts, and women in saris, trousers, dresses or salwaar kameez. But it's fun to see traditional clothing, isn't it? And it's just as good fun dressing up in traditional clothes for special occasions!

Autograph, please?

I have kept my autograph book ready. Daadu, will we meet many famous people?

We might. There are many famous people who are from Uttar Pradesh. But there are various well-known people from the past, who are not alive any more.

TULSIDAS

Tulsidas was the great poet and philosopher who wrote an epic called Ramcharitmanas. People say that the first word he uttered as a baby was 'Rama'.

VALMIKI

Valmiki was the learned sage who wrote the Ramayana.

VED VYASA

Ved Vyasa was another great sage, who wrote the Mahabharata.

AMIR KHUSRO

Amir Khusro was a poet who wrote many Sufi songs. Sufism is an Islamic movement.

SANT KABIR

Sant Kabir was a poet who wrote philosophical poems. They were always written in two lines and were called dohas. All our grandparents would know these for sure.

JAWAHARLAL NEHRU

Jawaharlal Nehru, who became India's first prime minister, was from Uttar Pradesh. He loved children. He was known as Chacha Nehru. We celebrate Children's Day in India on his birthday, 14 November.

BIRJU MAHARAJ

Birju Maharaj is one of the world's greatest Kathak dancers. He is also someone who made it popular for boys and men to learn classical dance.

MUNSHI PREMCHAND

Munshi Premchand was a famous writer who wrote lots of well-known books.

SITARA DEVI

Sitara Devi was also one of India's greatest Kathak dancers. Though she was born in Kolkata, her family came from Banaras.

DHYAN CHAND

Dhyan Chand was a famous hockey player and led India to many victories.

Jumble Tumble

These words are all jumbled up and Pushka is confused. Un-jumble them for him!

IKIMLAV — He wrote the Ramayana.

DEVYSVAA — He wrote the Mahabharata.

YAHDDNNCHA — A well-known hockey player who led India to many victories.

KAHTKA — The dance that Birju Maharaj and Sitara Devi are both famous for.

Once upon a time . . .

Uttar Pradesh is so interesting, Daadu. Are there any fun stories about the people who lived here?

Of course! The most famous ones are the stories of Akbar and Birbal. Birbal was a very clever minister in Emperor Akbar's court. There are hundreds of stories about Birbal's wit. Let me tell you one.

ANYTHING FOR MONEY

One day, Akbar was strolling in the gardens of his palace. He had a question he wanted to put to Birbal. He was thinking about how people do anything for money. He decided to ask Birbal his opinion, so he summoned him.

'Yes, Jahanpanaah,' Birbal said to his emperor, bowing low. 'What can I do for you?'

'Do you believe that people will do anything for money?' asked Akbar.

'If they are poor, and in need of money, then I am sure they will,' said Birbal.

'Let us put this to the test. Bring me a poor man and we'll see if this is true,' ordered Akbar.

The next day, Birbal brought a poor, thin Brahmin to meet Akbar. It was clear that the Brahmin had not eaten in a while. Akbar had thought of a task.

'Will you stand in the water of the Yamuna all night long? I will give you a bag of gold if you will do so,' Akbar told the poor Brahmin.

It was freezing, for it was the peak of winter. But at mention of the bag of gold, the Brahmin's eyes lit up. His family had not had food for a week.

'I will do it, Jahanpanaah,' the Brahmin replied.

That night, the poor Brahmin stood shivering in the cold river water all through the night. He was almost frozen. The next morning, he went to Akbar to claim his bag of gold.

'How did you manage to stand in such cold water?' Akbar demanded.

'Jahanpanaah, there was a lamp in the distance. I kept looking at the lamp and imagined that I could feel its heat. That gave me the strength to bear the cold,' the Brahmin replied.

'Aha! You did get heat from the lamp. No wonder you could stand the cold,' exclaimed Akbar. 'I cannot give you the gold, for you have cheated.'

The poor man could not do anything. He had to leave the court empty-handed. Birbal saw what had happened. He decided he must make Akbar realize his mistake.

The next day, Birbal told Akbar, 'Jahanpanaah, tomorrow I will bring you the most delicious khichdi in all the kingdom. I will make it myself.'

Akbar agreed happily. He loved khichdi.

For the next five days, there was no sign of Birbal in the court. Akbar got impatient.

'Where is Birbal, and where is my khichdi?' he said angrily. He decided to go to Birbal's house and see what Birbal was up to.

He ordered his men to saddle his horse. Soon, they reached Birbal's house. To Akbar's surprise, Birbal was sitting outside, in front of a cooking fire, but there was no vessel of khichdi. Instead, the vessel was hanging from a pole, at least ten feet higher than the fire.

'Oh, Jahanpanaah!' exclaimed Birbal. 'I am sorry it has taken so long. But the khichdi will be ready soon.'

'You are a fool,' shouted Akbar angrily. 'How do you expect the khichdi to be cooked when the fire is so far away from it?'

'Just like the Brahmin got heat from the lamp that was so far away,' replied Birbal.

Akbar immediately realized what Birbal was trying to tell him. He smiled to himself.

The very next day, he called the Brahmin to his court and gave him the promised bag of gold.

TRAVEL DIARY

Have you enjoyed this trip to Uttar Pradesh with your friends Mishki and Pushka—and, of course, with Daadu Dolma?

Now you can make your own Uttar Pradesh diary. And if you ever visit Uttar Pradesh, make sure you take pictures and put them in the photo box.

The first place I would visit in Uttar Pradesh:

_____

If I ever meet Akbar, this is what I would say to him:

_____

The one dish I am definitely going to eat:

_____

The monument that I find the most interesting:

_____

The one famous person from Uttar Pradesh I would love to meet:

_____

The dance I would love to learn:

_____

If I visited the Ganga, I would:

_____

The five words that I think describe Uttar Pradesh the best are:

_____

_____

_____

_____

_____

My Uttar Pradesh memories:

ANSWERS

page 9 HOT OR COLD

B

page 11 CITYSEARCH

A	L	A	G	O	M	T	I	A	W
V	R	I	N	D	A	V	A	N	F
A	G	E	R	M	Y	W	E	E	V
R	A	X	Y	N	O	X	C	V	N
A	N	V	G	W	D	Z	C	C	V
N	G	Z	N	J	H	A	N	S	I
A	A	E	B	A	Y	F	H	G	M
S	T	Q	R	Y	A	G	R	A	N
I	L	U	C	K	N	O	W	K	U
C	Y	A	M	U	N	A	R	R	W

page 15 WORD LADDER

Heather
Leather
Weather

page 17 HIDDEN WORDS

Here are some words you can make:
rat, nut, duct, data, chant, punch, patch, hard,
yam, ray, dam, drag, rag, hand, marry, curry,
guard, yard

page 23 MATCH THE WORDS

Salaam alaikum — Pranaam;
Janamdin mubarak — Saalgirah mubarak;
Aain na — Khushamdeed;
Khuda hafiz — Alvida; Ram ram — Khuda hafiz

page 25 TWIN SADHUS

B and D

page 29 ODD ONE OUT

Sports, Gazal, Nautanki, Ashoka

page 31 SONG BY THE RIVER

page 33 WINDOW DRESSING

Thirty-eight

page 35 COUNT THE DIAMONDS

Thirty-one

page 39 ROYAL MAZE

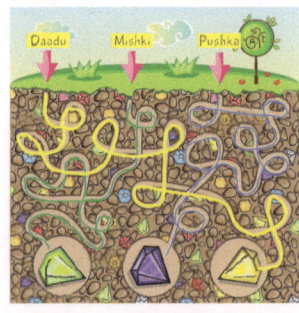

page 43 TOURIST TRICK

3

page 47 CRACK THE FOOD CODE

YUMMY HOT BIRYANI

page 53 JUMBLE TUMBLE

Valmiki, Ved Vyasa, Dhyan Chand, Kathak